MOTHER TERESA

www.pegasusforkids.com

© **B. Jain Publishers (P) Ltd.** All rights reserved. No part of this book may be reproduced, stored in a retrieval system or transmitted, in any form or by any means, mechanical, photocopying, recording or otherwise, without any prior written permission of the publisher.

Published by Kuldeep Jain for B. Jain Publishers (P) Ltd., D-157, Sector 63, Noida - 201307, U.P
Registered office: 1921/10, Chuna Mandi, Paharganj, New Delhi-110055

Printed in India

Contents

- 5   Who was Mother Teresa?
- 6   Her Childhood
- 10   The Call of Religion
- 16   The Mission Begins
- 24   Beginning of Missionaries of Charity
- 34   Missionaries of Charity-International
- 38   Declining Health
- 43   Awards and Accolades
- 47   Years of Suffering
- 50   Opinion of the Critics
- 54   Miracle and Beatification
- 56   The Glory of Mother Teresa
- 60   Character Traits of Teresa
- 62   Timeline
- 65   Activities
- 68   Glossary

Who was Mother Teresa?

Mother Teresa, the founder of the Missionaries of Charity, was a Roman-Catholic nun who is known all over the world as the supporter of the unwanted, unloved and neglected people around the world. One of the greatest humanitarians of the 20th century, she spent all her life serving the poorest of the poor, the aged, the unemployed, the diseased, the terminally ill, and those abandoned by their families. She was blessed with deep compassion, strong sense of commitment and love for the deprived and miserable fellow human beings. She along with her sisters of the Missionaries of Charity, clad in their blue bordered white saris, have become a symbol of love, hope and concern to millions around the world. She was honoured with the Nobel Peace Prize in 1979 for her service to humanity.

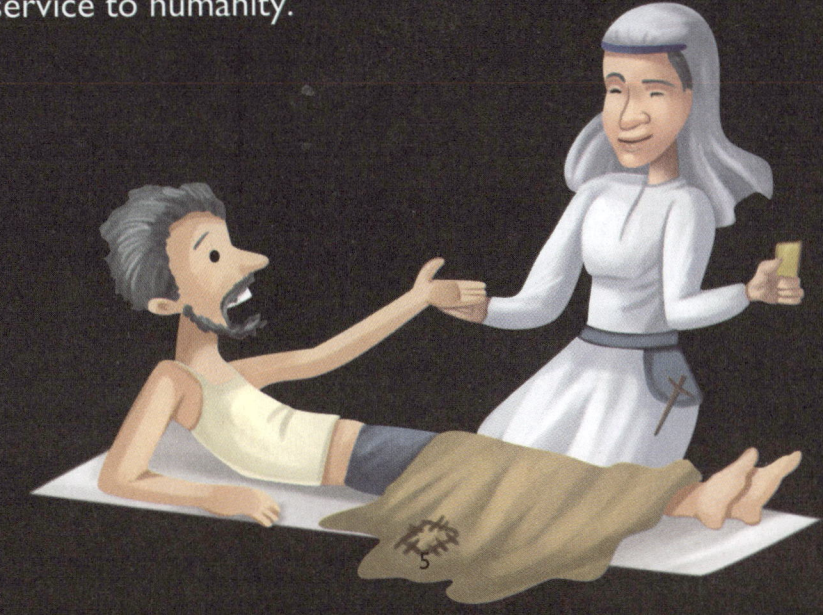

Her Childhood

Mother Teresa's original name was Agnes Gonxha Bojaxhiu and she was born in Skopje, now a part of the Republic of Macedonia, on August 26, 1919.

She was the youngest child of the three children born to the Albanian couple Nikollë and Drana Bojaxhiu. Her father was an entrepreneur by profession, who worked as a construction contractor and a trader of medicines and other goods. Hers was a deeply religious Catholic family. Her mother was a spiritual woman, who took

active participation in all the activities organized in the local church. Agnes received her First Communion when she was just five-and-a-half years of age.

This happy family was left shattered with her father's sudden and tragic death when she was just eight years old. While the cause of his death remains unknown, many suspect that political enemies poisoned him. After her father's death, Agnes became extraordinarily close to her mother, a pious and compassionate woman who instilled in her daughter a deep commitment to charity.

After her father's death, her mother raised her children as Roman Catholics. Despite facing very hard times, Drana did not compromise on the upbringing of her children; she raised them with utmost love, care and affection. Over the years, the affinity between Agnes and her mother grew more. Drana's spiritual and religious mind-set greatly influenced Agnes' character and her future profession.

Agnes grew up listening to the stories of the lives of missionaries with fascination. She learnt about their services in Bengal, India, and at the age of 12, she decided that she too would become a missionary and spread the love of Christ.

The Call of Religion

As a child, Agnes attended a convent-run primary school and then a state-run secondary school. As a young girl, she sang in the local Sacred Heart choir and was often asked to sing solos. The congregation made an annual pilgrimage to the Church of the Black Madonna in Letnice, and it was on one such trip at the age of 12 that Agnes first felt a calling to a religious life.

Six years later, in 1928, 18-year-old Agnes decided to become a nun and set off for Ireland to join the Sisters of Loreto in Dublin. Once there, she enrolled herself at the Institute of the Blessed Mary Virgin, also called 'Sisters of Loreto,' which also had missions in India. There she learnt English and received the name Sister Mary Teresa after St Therese of Lisieux. She never again saw her mother or siblings.

A year later, Sister Mary Teresa travelled to Darjeeling, India, for the novitiate period. In May 1931, she made her First Profession of Vows. Afterward she was sent to Kolkata, where she was assigned to teach at Saint Mary's High School for Girls, a school run by the Loreto Sisters. This school was dedicated to teaching girls from the city's poorest Bengali families. Sister Teresa learned to speak both Bengali and Hindi fluently. She taught geography and history, and dedicated herself to alleviating the girls' poverty through education.

On May 24, 1937, she took her Final Profession of Vows to a life of poverty, chastity and obedience. As was the custom for Loreto nuns, she took on the title of 'Mother' upon making her final vows and thus became known as 'Mother Teresa'.

Mother Teresa continued to teach at Saint Mary's, and in 1944 she became the school's principal. Through her kindness, generosity and unfailing commitment to her students' education, she sought to lead them to a life of devotion to Christ. "Give me the strength to be ever the light of their lives, so that I may lead them at last to you," she wrote in a prayer.

Mother Teresa was known in the convent for her love, kindness, compassion and generosity. A person devoted

to prayer and love for her sisters and her students, Teresa's 20 years in Loreto were filled with happiness. Noted for her charity, selflessness and courage, capacity to work hard, and a natural talent for organization, she lived a life dedicated to Jesus.

However, she was greatly disturbed by the poverty and misery that was prevalent in Kolkata and it seemed to increase with passing time.

She experienced two extremely distressing periods in Kolkata. The first was the Bengal famine of 1943, which had greatly affected the masses, especially the poor. The second was the Hindu-Muslim violence in 1946, before the partition of India. It added to the misery, despair and helplessness that Teresa saw around her.

The Mission Begins

Mother Teresa used to visit Darjeeling every year during the holidays. On September 10, 1946, she went to Darjeeling as usual for her annual retreat. She did not know that this visit would prove to be a turning point in her life. It transformed her life completely.

As she later described, Teresa experienced 'the call within the call' from the Almighty while travelling by train to the Loreto Convent in Darjeeling from Kolkata on September 10, 1946. "I was to leave the convent and help the poor while living among them. It was an order. To fail would have been to break the faith."

The Almighty had asked Mother Teresa to establish a new religious community, which would be dedicated to serving the 'poorest of the poor'. The community would work in the slums of Kolkata and help the poor and sick people.

Mother Teresa had taken a vow of obedience, and leaving the convent without official permission was impossible. For nearly two years, she campaigned for initiating the new religious community, and finally in January 1948, she was given approval to pursue the new calling by the local archbishop, Ferdinand Périer. Teresa began her missionary work with the poor in 1948.

On August 17, 1948, Teresa left the convent, which had been her home for almost two decades, and entered the world of the poor—a world that needed her, a world which He wanted her to serve, a world which was now her own!

She chose to wear a white Indian sari, with blue trimmings, out of respect for the traditional Indian dress.

Soon, Teresa adopted Indian citizenship and then spent a few months in Patna. Here, at the Holy Family Hospital, she received basic medical training. After completing her short course, Mother Teresa returned to Kolkata and found her temporary accommodation at Little Sisters of the Poor.

On December 21, 1948, Mother Teresa went out for the first time into the slums to help the people. Her primary mission was to serve the Lord by helping the 'unwanted, unloved, and uncared'. From then on, every day, Mother Teresa would go out into the city and reach out to the poor and needy. She just wanted to fulfill the Lord's desire to spread love, kindness and compassion.

Mother Teresa was soon joined by voluntary helpers in her noble mission. Most of them were former students and teachers, who joined her in her mission to fulfill His wish. With time, financial help also came in.

Initially, Mother Teresa started an open air school in Motijhil, Kolkata and soon established a home for the dying and destitute in a dilapidated home, which she convinced the government to donate to her.

In her diary Teresa wrote about her first year, which was filled with difficulties. She had no income. So, she often

begged for food and other supplies. She experienced doubt, loneliness and the temptation to return to the comfort of a convent life during this time.

For many years, Mother Teresa and a small band of fellow nuns survived on minimal income and food, often having to beg for funds. However, with time her efforts with the poorest were noted and appreciated by the local community and Indian politicians.

Beginning of Missionaries of Charity

On October 7, 1950, Teresa received permission from the Vatican to leave the Sisters of Loreto and start the 'Diocesan Congregation of the Calcutta Diocese,' which would later be famously known as the 'Missionaries of Charity'. In Mother Teresa's own words, this mission was to take care of 'The hungry, the naked, the homeless, the crippled, the blind, the lepers, and all those people who

feel unwanted, unloved, uncared for throughout society, people that have become a burden to the society and are shunned by everyone.'

This order began with only 13 members in Kolkata. The Missionaries of Charity went on to become one of the most significant and recognized congregations in the world. As the organization expanded, financial aid came in easily and Mother Teresa extended her scope for charitable activities.

Today, the order has more than 4,000 nuns, who run orphanages, AIDS hospices and charity centres worldwide. They have devoted their life to taking care of the refugees, the blind, disabled, aged, alcoholics, the poor and homeless, and victims of floods, epidemics, and famine.

In 1952, when Mother Teresa started her work with the dying destitutes, she was in desperate need of a place in which to care for them. She opened the first Home for the Dying, where people brought to this home received medical help and the right to die with dignity.

The local authorities of Kolkata offered her a section of the temple of Goddess Kali, which, though originally intended for the temporary housing of pilgrims, had become a hangout for thieves, drug addicts and pimps.

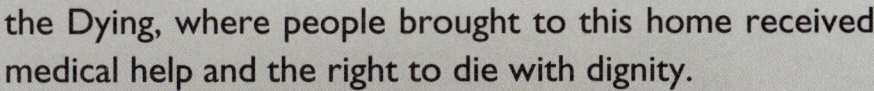

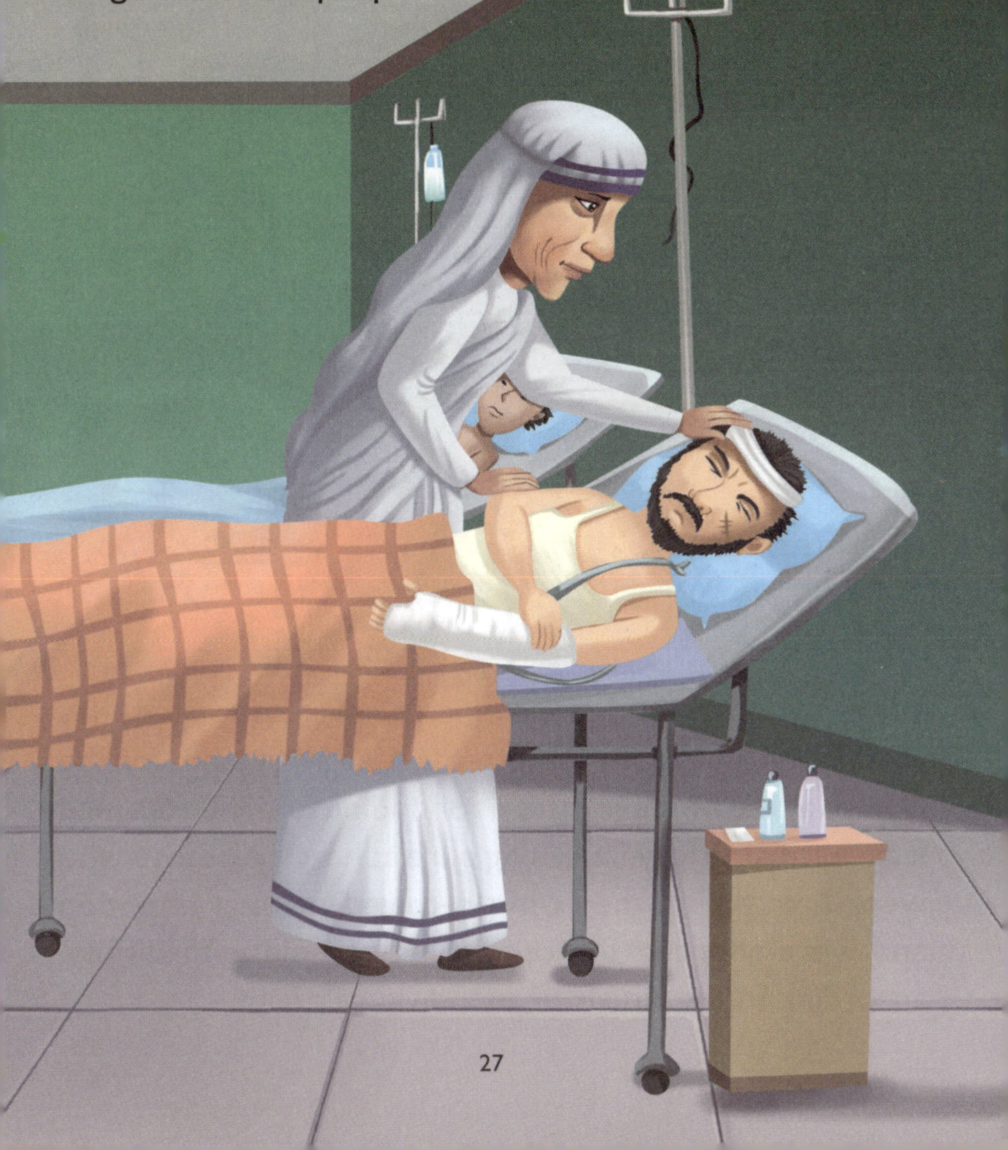

With the help of Indian officials, she converted this abandoned Hindu temple into the 'Kalighat Home for the Dying', a free home for the poor and needy. She renamed it as 'Nirmal Hriday,' meaning pure at heart. All those who were brought to the home received medical attention and were afforded the opportunity to die with dignity, according to the rituals of an individual's faith.

When the news circulated that the temple was being used by a woman and a foreigner and that she was trying 'to convert the poor to Christianity,' groups of people protested at the city hall. Others went to the nearest police station to demand that the woman be evicted. The police commissioner promised to do just that, but he first wanted to personally check things out.

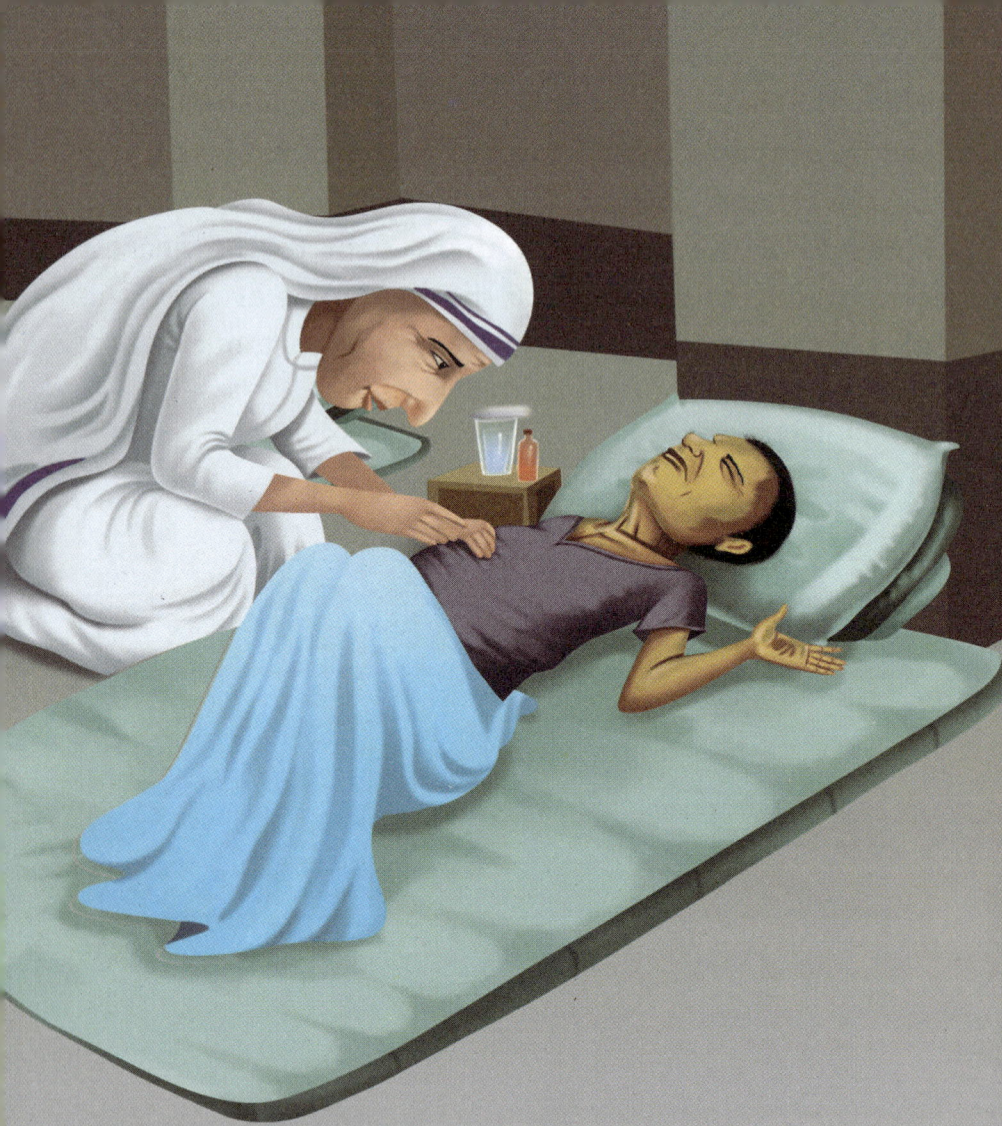

When the police commissioner went to see Mother Teresa, she was caring for a poor sick man by putting potassium permanganate on wounds from which worms were crawling out. The stench was unbearable.

Mother Teresa treated the officer with respect and offered to show him about. He answered that he preferred to look around on his own.

When he came out, he met some of the people who had complained about Mother Teresa and said, "I gave you my word that I would throw this woman out of here, and I would like to keep it. But, before I do so, you will have to get your mothers and sisters to do what she does. I make that the only condition for exercising my authority."

Mother Teresa soon opened a home for those suffering from leprosy. She named it the 'Hospice Shanti Nagar,' meaning City of Peace. Several other leprosy outreach clinics were also established by the Missionaries of Charity across Kolkata.

Mother's own words would define her service to the lepers when she said, "I try to give to the poor people for love what the rich could get for money. No, I wouldn't touch a leper for a thousand pounds; yet I willingly cure him for the love of God."

Also, as the Missionaries of Charity continued to take under their care many needy children, Mother Teresa decided to create a home for them as well. In 1955, she opened the 'Nirmala Shishu Bhavan' the Children's Home of the Immaculate Heart as a shelter for the orphans and homeless.

Abandoned children are of primary concern to the Missionaries of Charity. Mother Teresa's sisters do all they possibly can to make orphaned and abandoned children happy, even though they know that there is no substitute for real family. Mother Teresa once shared the following anecdote:

"One day, I discovered that a little one had lost his spark and his appetite after losing his mother. There was one Sister who looked like her, and the child would only smile and eat when he was near her. I entrusted the child to that Sister, after relieving her from her other duties for a few days. It did wonders for his health.

At times we can actually see happiness return to the lives of the dispossessed once they realize that many of us really care about them. And if they are sick, their health improves as well."

Mother's small efforts now quickly started growing in size and number. More and more people joined in and generous financial help started pouring in. By 1960, Missionaries of Charity had opened several hospices, orphanages and leper houses all over India.

In 1963, Missionaries of Charity Brothers was founded. The main aim behind the inauguration of Missionaries of Charity Brothers was to better respond to the physical and spiritual needs of the poor.

Missionaries of Charity-International

Gradually, Mother Teresa began to expand the order beyond the Indian borders. The Missionaries of Charities' first house outside India was opened in Venezuela in 1965 with five sisters. Other houses followed in Rome, Tanzania, and Austria in 1968. During the 1970s, the order opened houses and many foundations in various countries in Asia, Africa, Europe and the United States.

In 1976, a contemplative branch of the sisters was opened. Two years later, a contemplative brothers' branch was inaugurated. In 1981, Mother Teresa began the Corpus Christi Movement for Priests. In 1984, the Missionaries of Charity Fathers was founded by her in collaboration with Fr. Joseph Langford.

Mother Teresa then formed the Co-Workers of Mother Teresa, the Sick and Suffering Co-Workers, and the Lay Missionaries of Charity.

In 1982, during the Siege of Beirut, Mother Teresa rescued 37 children trapped in a frontline hospital while the cease fire between the Israeli army and Palestinian guerrillas was stopped for a temporary period. Accompanied by Red Cross workers, she travelled through the war zone to the devastated hospital and rescued its young patients.

It was also in the 1980s that Mother Teresa was able to build orphanages and hospices in eastern European countries that had previously refused her efforts.

She travelled to Armenia to help earthquake victims, the starving people of Ethiopia and the radiation-caused victims of Chernobyl. In 1988, after the Spitak earthquake, Mother Teresa visited the Soviet Republic of Armenia. She travelled to assist the hungry in Ethiopia, radiation victims at Chernobyl, and earthquake victims in Armenia.

The first Missionaries of Charity home in the United States was established in the South Bronx, New York. By 1984, it had 19 establishments all over the country.

By 1997, Missionaries of Charity had almost 4000 sisters working in 123 countries across the six continents. The congregation had several hospices and homes for people with HIV/AIDS, leprosy and tuberculosis, soup kitchens, children's and family counselling programmes, personal helpers, orphanages, and schools functioning under it.

In 1991, Mother Teresa returned to her homeland for the first time since 1937, and there she opened a Missionaries of Charity Brothers home in Tirana, Albania.

Declining Health

Mother Teresa's health started declining in the 1980s. She suffered a heart attack in Rome in 1983, when she had gone there to visit Pope John Paul II.

For the next couple of years, Mother Teresa faced constant health issues. She suffered a second heart attack in 1989. She was operated upon and received a pacemaker. In 1991, while she was in Mexico, she caught pneumonia which led to further heart problems. She offered to resign from her position as head of the Missionaries of Charity. However, the nuns of the order voted her as their head in a secret ballot. So, Mother Teresa continued to head the order.

In April 1996, Mother Teresa fell and broke her collar bone. In August, she suffered from malaria and failure of the left heart ventricle. She had a heart surgery but her health continued to decline.

Only months before her death, when she became too weak to manage the administrative work, she resigned from the position of head of her Missionaries of Charity on March 13, 1997.

Her last visit abroad was to Rome, when she visited Pope John Paul II for the second time.

After returning to Kolkata, Mother Teresa spent her last few days receiving visitors and instructing sisters so that

the organization could continue to run efficiently, even after her departure.

Finally, on September 5, 1997, after finishing her dinner and prayers, her weakened heart gave away and her soul was united with the Lord Almighty, who was the very core of her life. Her death was mourned by the entire world.

The former U.N. Secretary-General Javier Pérez de Cuéllar, mourning her death, said, "She is the United Nations. She is peace in the world."

At that time, Mother Teresa's Missionaries of Charity had over 4,000 sisters and an associated brotherhood of 300 members, operating 610 missions in 123 countries. These missions included hospices, soup kitchens, homes for people with HIV/AIDS, leprosy and tuberculosis, children's and family counselling programmes, orphanages and schools.

Mother Teresa lay in repose in St Thomas, Kolkata for one week before her funeral, which took place in September 1997. The Indian Government gave her a state funeral in gratitude for her services to the poor of all religions in India. She left a lasting impact on the next generation of missionaries and also on the world at large.

Until her death in 1997, Mother Teresa continued to work for and among the poorest of the poor, depending on God for all of her needs. Amazed by her care for those considered less fortunate, the deprived, and the ones usually thought of little value, the world showered her with numerous honours. In her own eyes she was, "God's pencil—a tiny bit of pencil with which he writes what he likes."

Despite years of fatiguing physical, emotional and spiritual work, Mother Teresa seemed unstoppable. Though fragile and bent, suffering with numerous ailments, she always returned to her work, to those who received her compassionate care for more than 50 years. She knew the work would go on.

Awards and Accolades

Mother Teresa was first recognized by the Indian Government, when she was awarded the Padma Shri in 1962 and the Jawaharlal Nehru Award for International Understanding in 1969.

In 1962, Mother Teresa received the Philippines-based Ramon Magsaysay Award for International Understanding. In 1967, she received the Pacem in Terris Award.

By the early 1970s, Mother Teresa had become an international celebrity. In 1971, she was awarded the first 'Pope John XXIII Peace Prize' for her work with the poor, display of Christian charity and efforts for peace.

In 1979, Mother Teresa was awarded the Nobel Peace Prize, 'for work undertaken in the struggle to overcome poverty and distress, which also constitutes a threat to peace.'

When Mother Teresa received the prize, she was asked, "What can we do to promote world peace?" She answered "Go home and love your family."

Building on this theme in her Nobel lecture, she said:

"Around the world, not only in the poor countries, but I found the poverty of the West so much more difficult to remove. When I pick up a person from the street, hungry, I give him a plate of rice, a piece of bread, I have satisfied him. I have removed that hunger. But a person that is shut out, that feels unwanted, unloved, terrified, the person that has been thrown out from society—that poverty is so hurtable and so much, and I find that very difficult to remove."

She refused the ceremonial banquet given to laureates, and asked that the US$ 192,000 funds be given to the poor in India, stating that earthly rewards were important only if they helped her to help the needy of the world. Mother Teresa was further honoured by various government and civilian organizations. In 1980, she received India's highest

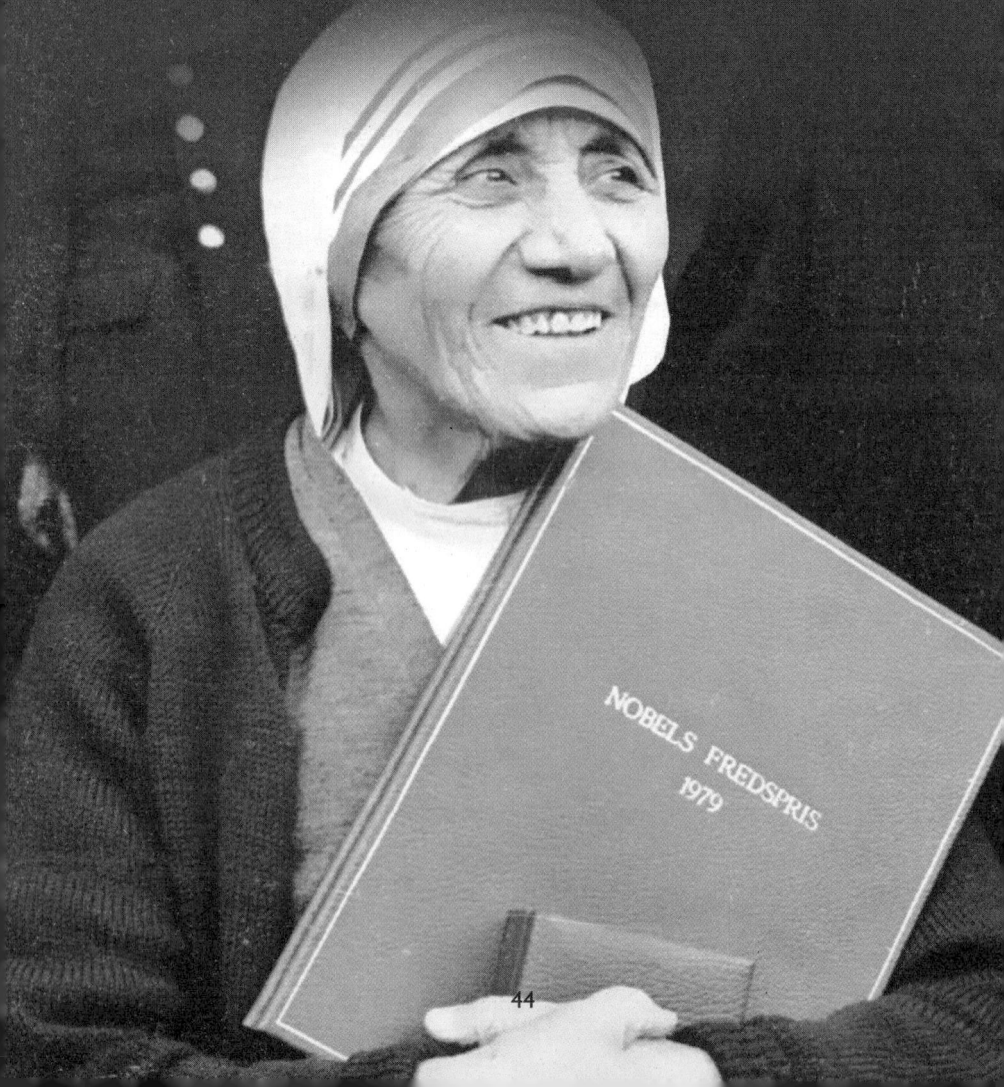

civilian award—Bharat Ratna. President Ronald Reagan presented Mother Teresa with the 'Presidential Medal of Freedom' at a White House ceremony in 1985.

The United Kingdom and the United States each repeatedly granted awards, culminating in the 'Order of Merit' in 1983, and 'Honorary Citizenship of the United States' received on November 16, 1996. Mother Teresa's Albanian homeland granted her the 'Golden Honour of the Nation' in 1994.

On August 28, 2010, honouring the 100th anniversary of her birth, the Government of India issued a special Rs. 5 coin. President Pratibha Patil said of Mother Teresa, "Clad in a white sari with a blue border, she and the sisters of Missionaries of Charity became a symbol of hope to many—the aged, the destitute, the unemployed, the diseased, the terminally ill, and those abandoned by their families."

Years of Suffering

Although Mother Teresa displayed cheerfulness and a deep commitment to God in her works but her letters indicate that she experienced doubts and struggles over her religious beliefs, which lasted nearly 50 years until the end of her life, during which "she felt no presence of God whatsoever ... neither in her heart or in the Eucharist".

Her letters reveal her suffering as she felt that Jesus has abandoned her as she began her new mission. Many have commented that her letters reveal her 'crisis of faith'. Her letters also express her immense pain over her

lack of faith. She wrote, 'Where is my faith? Even deep down ... there is nothing but emptiness and darkness ... If there be God—please forgive me.... How painful is this unknown pain—I have no Faith.' Despite this hardship, Mother Teresa retained her faith that God was working through her. She did not question his existence. However, it is believed by Catholics that these are spiritual tests experienced by many saints.

Mother Teresa described, after 10 years of doubt, a short period of renewed faith. At the time of the death of Pope Pius XII in 1958, praying for him at a requiem mass, she said she had been relieved of 'the long darkness: that strange suffering.' However, five weeks later, she described returning to her difficulties in believing.

Mother Teresa wrote many letters to her confessors and superiors over a 66-year period. She had asked that her letters be destroyed, concerned that 'people will think more of me—less of Jesus'. However, despite this request, the correspondences have been compiled in 'Mother Teresa: Come Be My Light.'

Mother Teresa was known as a great admirer of St. Francis of Assisi. Accordingly, her work and life show influences of Franciscan spirituality. The Sisters of Charity recite the peace prayer of St. Francis every morning during the Thanksgiving Communion and many of the vows and emphasis of her ministry are similar to the Franciscan order–to maintain chastity, obedience and submission to Christ.

Opinion of the Critics

Mother Teresa too faced her share of critics. As she became well known in the 1970s around the world, the number of her critics grew. Christopher Hitchens was one of her prominent critics. He believed that people were unable to examine what she did and therefore her reputation was mistaken!

There were a number of other critics who accused her of trying to convert people to Christianity and failing to provide accounts whereby the donors could know how their money was spent.

The support, recognition and donations she received also evoked criticism from some non-believers who thought that people innocently believed her and donated money willingly.

Some Bengali critics accused Mother Teresa of exploiting and even fabricating the degraded image of Kolkata in order to win international fame.

Allegations were made that she knowingly accepted donations from disreputable sources. It was said that in one notorious case she knew or ought to have known that the money was stolen; and that she accepted money from the autocratic and corrupt Duvalier family in Haiti, which she visited in early 1981. Although these allegations were

never proved, it did not stop her critics from repeating them.

The increasing wealth of the order she founded became yet another point of controversy. Questions were raised as to why her hospices were not renovated or the living conditions improved when the order was donated vast sums of money. While on the one hand, large sums were being spent on opening new convents and increasing missionary work, on the other, she did not apply donors' money on founding a modern medical facility in Kolkata, or transforming her Home for the Dying into a western-style hospice.

Two writers in the Western medical press in the mid-1990s commented that the approach to illness and suffering was not correct as it did not provide the facilities of modern medical investigations and medicines, and that the Home did not offer primary medical care, but only served as a refuge for the dying, with nowhere else to go.

She was also criticized for her view on suffering. She felt that suffering would bring people closer to Jesus. At a press conference during her October 1981 visit to Washington D.C., Mother Teresa stated, "I think it is very beautiful for the poor to accept their lot, to share it with the passion of Christ. I think the world is being much helped by the suffering of the poor people."

Miracle and Beatification

After Mother Teresa's death in 1997, there began the process of beatification—the third step towards possible canonization. This process requires the documentation of a miracle performed by the intervention of Mother Teresa.

In 2002, the Vatican recognized as a miracle the healing of a tumour in the abdomen of an Indian woman, Monica Besra, after the application of a locket containing Mother

Teresa's picture. There are disputed views about this 'miracle'. The Roman Curia, however, read through a number of works written about her life and works. The Vatican officials say that the Congregation for the Causes of Saints has found no obstacle to Mother Teresa's beatification.

The beatification of Mother Teresa took place on 19 October 2003, by Pope John Paul II at St Peter's Basilica, in Vatican City. Since then, she has been known as Blessed Mother Teresa. Along with Blessed Pope John Paul II, the Church designated Blessed Teresa of Kolkata as the patron saint of the World Youth Day.

The Glory of Mother Teresa

Mother Teresa has been immortalised and has been made patroness of various churches. There are also several roads and structures that have been named after Mother Teresa, including the International Airport of Alabama.

October 19 is celebrated as Mother Teresa Day in Albania and is observed as a public holiday. Her hometown, Skopje in Macedonia, has honoured Mother Teresa by opening the Memorial House of Mother Teresa in 2009. The Roman Catholic Cathedral in Pristina is also dedicated in her honour.

In India, where Mother Teresa spent her entire life in the service of poor, glowing tributes have been published in newspapers and magazines in her honour. Navin Chawla has showered her with compliments and praises in his biography, *Mother Teresa: The Authorized Biography*.

A new train, 'Mother Express,' which was introduced by the Indian Railways, was flagged off on August 26, 2010 to mark her birth centenary.

A charitable organization, 'Sevalaya,' runs Mother Teresa Girls Home, which provides free food, clothing, shelter and education to poor and orphan girls.

In 1984, the government of Tamil Nadu, India, opened Mother Teresa Women's University in Kodaikanal, Tamil Nadu to honour her.

Mother Theresa Post Graduate and Research Institute of Health Sciences, Puducherry has been established in 1999 by Government of Puducherry, India.

In 1969, a documentary titled 'Something Beautiful for God,' filmed by Malcolm Muggeridge, took her fame to a new level. He also published a book with the same title in 1971. During the filming of the documentary, the footage was taken in poor lighting conditions. The crew thought that they would not be able to use the footage. However, when the footage was later seen, it was found to be

extremely well lit. Muggeridge claimed this was a miracle of 'divine light' from Mother Teresa herself. However, the crew thought that it was due to a new type of ultra-sensitive Kodak film. Around this time, the catholic world too recognized her efforts.

In 1997, 'Mother Teresa: In the Name of God's Poor', won the Art Film Festival award. A 2003 Italian mini-series titled 'Mother Teresa of Calcutta,' which was re-released in 2007, received a CAMIE Award.

Mother Teresa's popularity has remained strong since her beatification.

The process leading up to the beatification has been the shortest in modern history—less than two years after Mother Teresa's death. Pope John Paul waived the normal five-year waiting period and allowed the immediate opening of her canonization cause.

"Her life of loving service to the poor has inspired many to follow the same path. Her witness and message are cherished by those of every religion as a sign that 'God still loves the world today,'" members of the Missionaries of Charity, the religious order she founded, said in a statement after Mother Teresa's beatification was announced.

Since her death, people have sought her help and have experienced God's love for them through her prayers. Every day, pilgrims from India and around the world come to pray at her tomb, and many more follow her example of humble service of love to the most needy, beginning in their own families.

Summing up her life in characteristically self-effacing fashion, Mother Teresa said, "By blood, I am Albanian. By citizenship, an Indian. By faith, I am a Catholic nun. As to my calling, I belong to the world. As to my heart, I belong entirely to the Heart of Jesus."

Mother Teresa will always be remembered for her selfless service to the poor, deprived, downtrodden, sick and the dying.

Character Traits of Teresa

Mother Teresa was the epitome of mercy and compassion. Her qualities have often been studied as follows:

Many people considered her humane due to the care she rendered to the people who needed help all around the world. She helped those who were suffering and showed utmost tenderness and sympathy towards them.

She was known to be very holy because of her great love for God. She never stopped thinking about Him and always kept Him in her heart. She had opened church houses in various countries so there would be a way that everybody would be able to hear of Christ.

She was a gracious person as she forgave easily. She never remembered the wrong things that people had done to her.

Determination was in the very nature of Mother. She always wanted to finish something she had started. In her childhood, every day she tried to remember to read the Bible, but forgot to do so many a times. However, she was determined to make it a habit and soon after, she was doing it every day.

Timeline

- 1910 August 26: Gonxha Agnes Bojaxhiu is born in Skopje (present-day Macedonia)
- 1910 She is baptised
- 1922–1923: At age 12, she feels the first call to religious life
- 1928 Mother Teresa leaves home to become a Roman Catholic Loreto nun and begins novitiate training in Dublin; she takes on the name Sister Teresa
- 1929 She arrives in Kolkata and becomes a teacher at St Mary's School
- 1931 She takes her first vow as a nun
- 1937 She takes final vows as a nun; becomes known as Mother Teresa
- 1946 On a train to Darjeeling, she receives 'the call within the call' to serve the poor
- 1948 Mother Teresa starts teaching poor children, opens her first slum school; shifts to 14, Creek Lane
- 1950 She founds the Missionaries of Charity with 12 sisters after getting the green signal from the Vatican
- 1951 She receives Indian citizenship

- 1952 She opens the first home for the dying at Kalighat in South Kolkata; names it Nirmal Hriday (Pure Heart)

- 1953 Mother Teresa leaves Creek Lane and shifts to a two-storeyed building on Lower Circular road. Now it is called Mother House, the global headquarters of the Missionaries of Charity

- 1957 She begins her work with lepers for which her order becomes well known around the world

- 1962 The Indian Government honours her with the Padma Shri award for her humanitarian work

- 1963 Mother Teresa begins Missionaries of Charity, Brothers

- 1965 The Catholic Church grants her permission for setting up missions outside India; the first opens that year in Venezuela

- 1971 She receives Pope John XXIII Peace Prize and uses the money to build a leper colony

- 1976 Mother begins Missionaries of Charity, Contemplative Sisters

Timeline

- **1979** She founds Missionaries of Charity, Contemplative Brothers
- **1979** She is awarded the Nobel Peace Prize for her work with the destitute and the dying
- **1980** She receives India's highest civilian honour—Bharat Ratna
- **1982** Mother Teresa rescues 37 mentally disabled children from a hospital in besieged Beirut
- **1983** She visits Pope John Paul II; she is hospitalized with heart attack, the first of several to follow.
- **1984** She begins Missionaries of Charity Fathers
- **1985** She is awarded the Medal of Freedom, the highest US civilian honour
- **1990** Mother Teresa resigns as superior general of the Missionaries of Charity but is re-elected
- **1997** She steps down as head of her order
- **1997** She dies of heart failure in Kolkata at age 87
- **2003** Mother Teresa is beatified by Pope John Paul II, placing her a step from sainthood

Class Discussion

What is your idea of the word 'service'? Have a group discussion with your classmates and teacher. Your discussion should include the following points:

- Where should you start service from?
- How will you know who needs your help?
- At this stage when you all are very young, what are the kind of services that you can provide to society and your country at large?

A Visit

The teacher should plan a visit to any one of the homes of Mother Teresa in the city they live in.

Group Activity

In groups of five, collect pictures of Mother Teresa doing her different services in different parts of the world. Make a collage with it.

Activities

Activities

Questions

1. Who was Mother Teresa?
2. What was Mother Teresa's real name?
3. Name her parents.
4. When and where was Mother Teresa born?
5. What did her father do?
6. Describe the nature of Agnes' mother.
7. Where and when did Agnes take her first professional vows?
8. When and where did Agnes take the title of 'Mother'?
9. Name the school of which she became the principal in Kolkata.
10. Give four adjectives to describe Mother Teresa.
11. What did Mother mean by 'a call within a call'?
12. When did Mother finally begin her missionary work?
13. What did Mother and her nuns choose to wear when they began their mission in Kolkata? Why?

14. When did Missionaries of Charity begin?

15. How many members did it have initially?

16. Name some of the other organizations which Mother Teresa began to help the poor.

17. When was Missionaries of Charity Brothers founded?

18. Name the countries outside India where Mother Teresa started working.

19. When and why did Mother Teresa get the Nobel Prize?

20. Name some of the other important awards she was honoured with.

21. What were the illnesses that Mother Teresa suffered from?

22. When did she breathe her last?

23. What are the values you think Mother Teresa left for us to understand?

Glossary

abandoned: having been left

accommodation: a place or building in which someone may live

admirer: someone who has a particular liking for someone or something

alcoholics: relating to alcohol

anniversary: a date on which an event took place

beatification: declaration by the Pope of the Roman Catholic Church that a dead person is in a state of bliss, constituting a first step towards canonization

Black Madonna: a Black Madonna or Black Virgin is a statue or painting of Mary in which she is depicted with dark skin

campaign: a series of military operations intended to achieve a goal

chastity: to maintain a pure character

commitment: the state of being dedicated to a cause

compassion: pity or concern for the sufferings of others

compassionate: a person who feels for others

congregation: a group of people assembled for religious worship

Glossary

construct: to make a building or industrial product

contemplative: thoughtful or to be devoted in prayer

contractor: a person or firm that undertakes a contract to provide materials or labour for a service

counselling: professional assistance and guidance in solving personal or psychological problems

deprived: suffering a severe lack of basic material needed for living

destitute: very poor

devastated: to get destroyed

dignity: the quality of being worthy of honour

diseased: a person who is suffering from a disease

documentary: pertaining to documents

downtrodden: people who are treated badly by people in power

epidemic: an infectious disease which has widely spread

Eucharist: the Christian service, ceremony, or sacrament commemorating the Last Supper

famine: extreme scarcity of food

Glossary

fascination: the power to fascinate someone

funeral: a ceremony or service held shortly after someone's death gratitude: to be thankful

generosity: the quality of being kind and open in giving things to others

hospices: a home providing care for the sick or terminally ill

humane: having or showing compassion or kindness

humble: having or showing a low estimate of one's importance

inauguration: the beginning of a system, policy, or period

inspired: something arising from some external creative impulse

investigation: a formal or systematic examination

laureate: a person who is honoured with an award for outstanding achievement whether creative or intellectual

leprosy: a contagious disease that affects the skin

miracle: an extraordinary happening

missionaries: a person sent on a religious mission to promote Christianity in a foreign country

obedience: to carry out an order or request

Glossary

opportunity: a set of circumstances that makes it possible to do something

orphanages: a place where the children with missing parents are cared for

patroness: a female patron

pilgrimage: a journey to a holy place

pneumonia: lung inflammation caused by bacterial or viral infection

potassium permanganate: a purple-brown solid (intensely purple in solution) used as an oxidizing agent and in chemical analysis

poverty: the state of being extremely poor

pursue: to follow or chase someone or something

radiation: the emission of energy as electromagnetic waves

repose: a state of rest or sleep

Requiem Mass: also known as Mass for the Dead is a Mass in the Catholic Church offered for the repose of the soul

selflessness: one who is concerned with the needs and wishes of others

significant: quite important

Glossary

slums: an overcrowded urban street inhabited by very poor people

spirituality: relating to God

temptation: the desire to do something wrong

tuberculosis: an infectious bacterial disease characterized by the growth of nodules or tubercles in the tissues

unemployed: a person who does not have a job

ventricle: a hollow or cavity in an organ